THE BLUFFER'S GUIDES

D0766723

THE BLUFFER'S GUIDES

Published or in preparation

BLUFF YOUR WAY IN ANTIQUES

ANDRÉ LAUNAY

Published by The Bluffer's Guides
335 Kennington Road, London SE11 4QE

(01) 582 4887

General Editor – Peter Gammond
Series Editor – Anne Tauté

Cover design – Jim Wire
Typesetting – John Buckle (Printers) Ltd.
Printing & Binding – Hunt Barnard Printing Ltd.

For the objects on the cover, grateful thanks are due to:

Kears of Kennington, Windmill Row,
London SE11 (Georgian wine glass c.1740;
Georgian decanter c.1800.)

Antiques, 300 Kennington Road,London SE11
(Victorian silver sugar sifter; Georgian silver snuff box
by William Bateman; Silver caddy spoon c.1790;
Victorian cameo mounted in jet.)

CONTENTS

INTRODUCTION

A thing of beauty is a joy for ever.
Its loveliness increases . . .

So does the price. This is the simple basis upon which
the whole world of Antiques – buying, having and
selling – is based. There are a few people who like to use
antiques; but most would prefer to sit on a comfortable
modern chair in a modern centrally-heated home while
listening to their digital discs on modern hi-fi equipment. For most people it is not particularly practical to
have bits of Ming sitting around on the sideboard within
reach of children and animals.

Antiques are mainly things that change hands,
costing a bit more each time they change. Since the
early 1970s when the BBC in Bristol (home of Bristol
delftware, Bristol glass and Bristol porcelain) trans-
mitted a series of programmes showing expert dealers
examining various chairs, chests, glasses and spoons
with palpable awe – and then pricing them way beyond
the average pocket – viewers have been rushing up to
attics and ferretting around in cellars, to unearth long-
lost and sometimes best-forgotten bits of bric-à-brac,
convinced that, because they are older than they are
themselves, they must be worth a fortune.

The disdain with which the hoped-for buyers handle
these family heirlooms and declare them to be Victorian
reproductions of no particular value, frequently stuns
the owners into temporary silence and a permanent
lack of faith in humanity. It also awakens a desire to be
knowledgeable on the subject so that dealers and
doubters can be put in their rightful place.

This slim volume may not turn you, overnight, into a

walking encyclopaedia of antiques, but it will help you to remain articulate when you walk into an antique shop or able to hold your own when the dinner conversation turns, as it inevitably does, to the subject of personal wealth and acumen.

In fact, all you need know about antiques is that they should be rare, unrestored and in perfect condition; but it will help to be able to throw in a few words like *epergné, marquetry* and *remboitage,* or to know your oak from your ash. The world of antiques is rich in bluffers and bluffing. Step in.

ANTIQUE DEALERS

There are a number of certain ways of losing money. Buying antiques is one of them.

Enter an antique shop in the wrong frame of mind and you are bound to come out believing you have a bargain, when all you have done is to increase your overdraft and confirm your bank manager's opinion that you are an idiot.

The approach is all-important when you decide to buy an antique. Leave behind your pride and any show of wealth. The well-dressed, well-motored customer is doomed from the start. Antique dealers look at your shoes and accessories before they look at the whites of your eyes. They can tell at a glance what sort of sucker you are. Bare feet or sandals in winter, snowboots in summer will throw them for a bit. A well-practised expression of disappointment at the show of objects on sale will get you a discount – except in Mayfair where there is an exception to every rule.

The main thing, wherever you are, is to be as acute as the dealers. To be that, it is essential to sum them up within seconds of entering their kingdom. The following guide should help.

Basically there are two definite types of antique dealers: the amateur and the professional.

The professionals regard the amateurs with mixed feelings. On one hand they are useful persons on whom they can unload all their unwanted junk at a good profit. On the other hand they get in the way at auctions, bidding at the wrong moment and putting up the prices quite unnecessarily.

It is wrong to believe that dealers compete with one another. Very much the contrary. They are a strong brotherhood, united in the cause of ruining everyone except themselves. Once they have done that they may start cutting each other to pieces, but that day has not yet come.

If one dealer, whether amateur or professional, advises you against going to another's shop, it is not because he is a rotten cad trying to stop a competitor getting a new customer. It is because he knows his colleague wouldn't be able to put up with your unceasing chatter on fuddling cups, and that you are not likely to spend more than the £2 you have spent with him on a broken papier mâché matchbox holder (worth all of 50p) supposedly Georgian. If it is not 'Georgian' by the way, then it's bound to be 'Victorian'. Few dealers risk acknowledging other periods.

A fuddling cup, in case you don't know, is a cup with three, five or six conjoined compartments communicating internally, made in slipware at Donyat and Crock Street in Somerset, between 1697 and 1770. If you don't know what slipware is, we suggest you buy an encyclopaedia of antiques. You can't expect a modest book like this to tell you everything.

THE AMATEURS

The Amateur antique dealer is easily recognisable and quite different from the professional. He comes in two distinct models – the Rich and the Poor.

The Rich ones are mean because they are collectors at heart, hate parting with their goodies, and don't really have to. The Poor are mean because they can't afford to be anything else.

Both have a private income on which they rely for food. Their status as dealers depends entirely on how much of that income they pour into the business.

The Rich amateur antique dealer is the easiest to find. There is one in every country town within earshot of the hunting horn, two or three in every double-glazed village dotted in the green belt, and hundreds cleverly hidden in remoter parts, usually surrounded by glorious windswept views.

These places are advertised in the fashionable antique magazines with all the pretence of social standing one could wish for. The shop will be a converted barn or parish-room situated within the grounds of a large converted farmhouse or old rectory. Outside, a sign in gothic letters will hang from a cleverly adapted bit of wrought iron, and inside there will be wonders to brighten the eyes of any collector – Grandma's sporting prints, Aunty's collection of Victorian silhouettes, glasses galore with all the beautiful defects mentioned at some time or other by Peter Lazarus. If you really want to sound knowledgeable about glass anywhere in the British Isles just mention his name, or that of William Meadows, and see what happens.

In the place of honour, a fireplace fitted with glass shelves and floodlit, or a Victorian bath hung sideways on the wall and used as a display cabinet, will be the highly prized genuine pieces of porcelain in prime condition. All of which can be bought for a slightlier lower price at Sothebys or Christies where they came from originally.

Under the genuine looking pieces of furniture will be found subtle price codes, indecipherable to the au-pair assistant, or a 'confidential' bit of information about it

11

which will have been gathered from various old books after a great deal of research; and which may be totally wrong.

Don't buy here except in the opening week when the owners won't know what they are doing and will be so frightened at actually having to 'take' money that they might give something away if you admire it enough. This pleasant attitude towards commerce, however, will be short-lived.

The Poor amateur antique dealer does not trade with such panache. He is an intellectual with an Oxford or Cambridge degree in philosophy – which is why he is able to stand the life.

He has no shop, but a garage or shed next to his widowed mother's derelict house. In it he has failed for years to repair, strip or re-varnish the vast quantities of useless furniture he has bought cheaply at market auctions, but he knows that his stock, once done up, will be worth a fortune.

He spends most of his time at such auctions scoffing at his richer colleagues for buying rubbish he can't afford, and therefore is seldom 'at home'. When he is, a bargain may be found inside a damp and mouldy Victorian (or Georgian) sideboard, or under a collapsed Chesterfield which had the stuffing taken out of it when it fell off the roof of his rusty Renault 5. Such bargains will range from chipped rummers (see Glass) for £1 each to brass candle snuffers for £1.50.

Brass purchased from Poor amateur antique dealers takes approximately 17½ days of continual hard rubbing to get clean.

THE PROFESSIONALS

There are a number of different categories under this heading which can be narrowed down to six distinguishable types. All have one important thing in common – the fact that antiques are their bread and butter. They have to make a profit on everything in order to eat and pay the rent.

A professional's success is due not only to astute dealing, but also – and much more – to knowledge. It is the man at an auction who spots that a table is a genuine walnut William and Mary when everyone else believes it to be a reproduction, or can confidently date a piece of silver because he knows the marks, who wins the day. Such knowledge can only be acquired by study and experience in the trade, and the people who have it deserve whatever small fortune occasionally comes their way – which is all the support they're going to get from us.

We shall start in the bargain basement:—

The Market Stall Holder

This stall is usually found in a small country town laden with cracked tea-pot lids, three copies of *War and Peace*, Vol. 2, a stack of *Illustrated London News* (1935), pressed flowers framed with Victorian love, dusty heatproof dishes and a vast quantity of plastic kitchen utensils and toys.

Behind the stall, you will find either a dirty old man (in every sense of the word), an extremely refined lady in a moth-eaten fur coat who once knew the Duke of Windsor personally, or the wife of the greengrocer on the next stall.

Don't waste your time looking. Fifteen years ago an occasional bargain might have been found on such stalls, but not any more. Whenever stall holders get hold of something good they sell it directly to a richer dealer before they start their day's work. Such a sale *is* a day's work, which accounts for so many stalls never opening at all.

The Country Town or Village Antique Shop

This is a different copper kettle of fish. In such places top antique dealers-to-be learn the tricks of *the* Trade.

Here, reasonably knowledgeable people have had sufficient business acumen to start trading. They are successful either because they do not charge exorbitant prices – keeping to an SPQR policy (small profit quick return) – or have perfected the art of buying their stock cheaply. Such people come in different shapes and sizes, the most popular being the young man who gives you the impression that you are much cleverer than him, and so *very* artistic that a certain objet d'art he has had hanging around since he opened could be beautifully converted, only by you, into something 'frightfully improbable but gosh what fun!'

When he buys (either something you have brought to his shop to sell, or invited him to see at home) he will glance at it with great disdain to make you realize straight away that he couldn't possibly ruin his aesthetic senses by having such a thing on his premises.

He will, however, admire something you don't value, buy it for an unexpected price, then offer you a little something for the piece you originally wanted to sell – because he 'doesn't want to disappoint you'.

A year or so later you will learn that 'the piece' was worth a bomb and that he sent it straight to a collector in Geneva.

The Home Counties Set

In the oppressive and over-civilized areas, where colourful plastic gnomes and daily weeded crazy-paving are seen in the company of white painted wheelbarrows overflowing with trailing geraniums and pair upon pair of carriage lamps hanging on either side of front doors with bell chimes, the collector can meet his doom.

Antique shops in such places are spotlessly clean, smell of lavender furniture polish, have real flowers neatly arranged in a reproduction 17th century pewter tavern pot – and display outrageous prices.

Genteel middle-aged, middle-class ladies, with blue hair and fob bracelets, will look down their noses at you through American-style tinted spectacles. They know nothing about antiques and will make no attempt to sell you anything.

If you are sufficiently rude you may get to know the price of a horse brass or two. But what you are really expected to do is walk in and say, 'I'll have that Welsh Dresser, that piece of Staffordshire and that paperweight', sign a cheque without batting an eyelid, watch them being expertly wrapped in pink tissue paper (she once worked in a major department store), and give the address to which the dresser might be delivered in three months time if you're lucky.

It is honestly cheaper to go to Harrods where reproductions are sold as such and not mixed up with genuine antiques for the unsuspecting to get landed with.

The Lord at the Manor

Somewhere in every county there is a large stately home, Elizabethan, Tudor or Georgian (never Victorian in this case), surrounded by well-maintained gardens, with a sweeping drive leading through crested wrought-iron gates to the entrance steps flanked by stone Grecian statues, Egyptian lions, or 14th century cannons with their balls neatly piled near at hand.

The atmosphere outside is impressive enough, but once through the massive studded oak doors you are floored by the abundance of luxury. Everywhere you look there are antiques of priceless value, chandeliers, furniture, ornaments, paintings and carpets. They all seem to be here and all are for sale – for these are the premises of an antique dealer – wholesale.

If you are not in 'the Trade' you will not be too welcome. This is not the sort of place to ask for a pot-lid or a ladder-back chair. A dozen of the first perhaps, or six sets of the second maybe, but if you are told in no uncertain terms that they are closed to tourists, you must not take umbrage. You would not, after all, go to Smithfield to buy one lamb chop.

The man who runs such an establishment is usually well into his sixties, bent with arthritis (there is no central heating because it is bad for the furniture) and round-shouldered from hours spent counting money stored in coffers (pieces of eight, dubloons, he's not fussy).

If you are extremely knowledgeable on one particular subject which happens to interest him (19th century cigar cases, pre-1850 toys, Minton portrait busts) and can talk and get genuinely excited about his private collection, then you may become his friend for life.

This does not mean that you will get a discount on anything (antiques are his bread and butter as previously mentioned), but you may actually be invited into the inner sanctum – his own private living quarters hidden somewhere dim at the back of the mansion. And there you will get a surprise.

Does a fishmonger chew smoked salmon all day? Does a greengrocer pick for himself the juiciest fruit on which he is likely to make most profit? No. To them it would be like eating money. Wholesale antique dealers are the same.

Their homes are inexpensively furnished with modern sideboards and bedroom suites, chrome-plated television sets, tiled fireplaces, even china ducks chasing china drakes diagonally across the wall – but never any saleable antiques.

If you get shown the basement of the mansion, a privilege indeed, you'll find it a hive of industry. Here, a number of men will be fully employed packing Breakfast Bookcases, Lowboys, Escritoires and Whatnots by the gross . . . for shipment to America.

Treat wholesale antique mansions such as these as museums, unless you go with a large cheque book and a small pantechnicon.

The Fulham and/or Harrow Road

There is a type of shop which has been established in certain roads leading westwards from the centre of London for many years. They seem from the outside to deal in interesting antiques. They don't. Inside you may find an unstrung harp, or an empty grandfather clock case. It is a mystery how such places exist. By all means look in, but don't expect to buy anything.

The Portobello Road
or Giant Confidence Trick

For about five hours every Saturday morning the world meets his wife in the Portobello Road. It is probably the only place on earth where everyone tries to rook everyone else, and generally succeeds.

Customers bargain like crazy with stall holders when they have never bargained before, and then sell what they have just bought to other stall holders for a profit, who in turn sell to other customers who repeat the process all the way down the road, or up, till a scent bottle which started off that morning at 50p, ends up in the original seller's wife's hands for £30, knocked down from £35.

Here professional dealers lose their heads trying to compete with the baffling ignorance of the amateur. Tourists can be seen leaving the area loaded with yesterday's supply of new Edward VII/Queen Alexandra coronation mugs, while chi-chi Londoners search in vain for £5 flowered chamber pots to use as salad bowls, or chinese snuff bottles to hang on the end of lavatory chains.

You may hear that in the early morning, at 7.30 a.m., the knowledgeable antique dealers scout round the stalls before they open to the public and buy up all the bargains worth having. Do not believe a word of it: the only reason some dealers go there early is to have a jolly good breakfast of ham and eggs with friends in the trade.

The Mayfair Set

In or just off Bond Street, Mount Street and Sloane Street.

You have to have special training to walk into one of these showrooms. Calling them 'shops' may well disqualify you from entering any of them, unless the word 'shop' is used as a term of amused endearment, much as the Queen might refer to Sandringham as 'the country cottage'.

If you haven't got a double-barrelled name, make one up. Dress expensively but soberly. Women should wear hats, men should remove theirs on entering, and children should never be seen or heard.

Arrive in a chauffeur-driven limousine, taxi, or gold plated mini. Never talk money or ask a price. Admire and buy, or get out. Refrain from picking up the Georgian silver cigarette box which is *not* for sale, but placed there, full, for RELIABLE customers only.

If you imprudently decide to buy anything, do not ask for your purchases to be wrapped or expect to be allowed to take them away. Everything is sent to your London address – whether you've got one or not.

Antique Fairs

These are not medieval fiestas with stocks, maypoles or orange sellers, but special weeks during which top antique dealers in certain areas exhibit their best pieces in one place, more often than not the ballroom of the local five-star hotel.

The motor industry does something similar. It's not only another excuse to have a jolly booze-up behind an 18th century Italian leather screen but a clever way of getting even more foreigners to come and buy Britain's past.

It is also an extremely good way for you to kill with one stone a large number of Meissen birds.

The Antique Supermarket

Antique supermarkets derive their origin from the Portobello Road indoor markets, and are run on the same principle.

An old warehouse, theatre, department store, basement or church is bought by some enterprising young person who partitions off as many little cubicles as possible in the space available, then lets this space off for as much as possible.

These spaces are the 'stalls' and they are rented for a day, week, month or year either by amateur dealers who have not had the capital to buy a shop, or by professionals who may have a business in the country or in another part of town, and who wish to sell some of their stock to new faces.

The supermarkets are much abused because many of the stalls purport to sell antiques when in fact they sell everything but: Harry Roy 78s, old sheet music, 1914-18 helmets and uniforms bought in bulk from the props of 'war films', and other strange collectors' items which are often a lot younger than the people selling them.

The excitement of looking for a bargain still exists in such places, and occasionally a find may be found.

The Antique Hypermarket

The Hypermarket caters for the jet-set collector, the person in a hurry who only has time to walk round the stalls once, yet who can be sure that what he purchases is genuine – for there is an implied guarantee that whatever is sold on the premises is a true antique. (See note on True Antiques.)

Such a place is not recommended to the person who does not know what he is looking for – but it is a most enjoyable way to kill time on a rainy day.

PRIVATE ANTIQUE COLLECTORS

There are no public antique collectors.

All antique collecting is done in private, either in the depths of an early provincial style Louis XV corner cabinet, on the chimney piece, or hanging from walls.

Private Antique Collectors unlike dealers, are very unfriendly towards each other. They are jealous, mean and sometimes exceedingly nasty. As far as they are concerned the only purpose other collectors serve is in amassing, over a number of years, a quantity of interesting objects which will eventually be sold, thus giving *them* a chance to amass, over a number of years, a similar quantity of interesting objects which they will eventually sell, thus giving *other* collectors a chance to amass . . . and so ad infinitum.

When buying from a collector, remember that you are buying part of his or her life.

You may be interested in a pair of Walton figures (made by John Walton in pottery from 1810 to 1835 with tree backgrounds decorated with bright enamel colours and black). You have heard of a pair which an elderly lady may sell. You are going to take a bit of her, a part of her life, away. Your approach, therefore, must be kind and respectful, not as though you were going to take her pet dog to the vet to be put away because it bit the postman, but as though you were personally going to take care of her pet dog *despite* the fact that it bit the postman.

Money is not what matters most to a collector. A good home for the favourite item is more important. You must therefore convey that you are a provider of good homes for Bracket Clocks, Lambeth Tiles, Caughley Teapots or whatever. Any hint that you might in time sell them could totally ruin your purchasing power.

THE TRADE DISCOUNT

To the question 'Are you Trade?' Always answer un-flinchingly 'Yes!'

You will then get a discount. If you answer 'no' it will be generally believed that you have enough money not to care what you are charged.

Antique dealers do more trade between themselves than with private customers. Their prices are therefore calculated to make the necessary profit with the trade but, as there is always a chance of making that extra bit with the private customer, the private customer's price is quoted.

Dealers always make it known that they are 'Trade' before asking a price. They are then quoted the private customer's price less about 10 per cent, or even more – whatever the selling dealer thinks he can knock off without ruining himself.

To be 'Trade' means that you buy antiques to re-sell them, making a profit on the transaction. Whether you re-sell the pieces that day, within a week, a month, a year or ten years is irrelevant. If you buy to re-sell, you are 'Trade' and as you are bound to re-sell sooner or later, there is nothing to stop you calling yourself 'Trade', except the pride of not wanting to be associated with the dealing world.

AUCTIONS

As with shops and dealers there are different categories of auctions – good and terrible.

Unlike shops and stalls, however, there is a sporting chance of getting a bargain at an auction, providing you can keep your head.

Market Town Auctions

Once a week, or maybe more, an auction is held in most country towns to sell off the accumulated flotsam of someone's life – someone who has sold up and left the area, or someone who has joined the heavenly choir.

Such sales take place in a saleroom, or in some kind of hall like The Corn Exchange or The Produce Market. Among the paraffin stoves and early 20th century refrigerators and typewriters, threadbare carpets and rusty lawnmowers, a piece of porcelain or pottery might be found. This is rare, but it can happen. When it does, ten to one a dealer with a wodge of banknotes too heavy to carry in a Gladstone bag (1872), will be there to outbid you.

If you really have nothing better to do, an occasional visit to the 'viewing' before the sale is worth while. If your time is limited, don't bother with this type of auction, or the next one either.

No 23 Acacia Avenue

'Sale of antiques and household effects'

In the Spring and Autumn when everyone's fancy turns to a change of environment, estate agents are frantically busy selling houses for less than they are worth, and auctioneers are frantically busy selling the contents. Sometimes these small 'residential' auctions are interesting. Most of the time they are deadly.

Houses in suburbs are unlikely to be of great interest to the keen collector, but small cottages lost in the country, or farmhouses/terrace houses in once-wealthy mining towns can be very rewarding – especially if a family has been living there for generations. Here, a print or a bit of Staffordshire or Derby which was given to Grandpa a hundred years ago, will have gained in value and maybe escaped the notice of the locals.

Such auctions, unfortunately, are the life-blood of the amateur antique dealer, and it is more than likely that you will get two rivals bidding for a Georgian musical box (in fact made in Japan 1926) and taking it up to an astronomical figure purely for emotional reasons. This invariably results in everyone catching the 'I can outbid anyone' disease. The remaining lots will not go for a song but for an anthem – and a national one at that.

If you have seen what you want when viewing and can set a price on it and not go above it, then such an auction is worth a trip. If you are an extrovert you will, of course, ruin yourself.

The Country House Sale

The sale will be announced in the Sunday heavies, the *Times, Guardian* and *Telegraph* and antique magazines. It will also be advertised on posters stuck in unlikely places. Well-known dealers will be sent details by post.

The first thing to do is go to the viewing. This will take place one, two or three days before the auction, which itself may be spread over two or three days depending on the number of lots.

The house itself will be up for sale as well, so you can wander around at your leisure poking your nose into someone else's past. The place is yours until the new owners take over.

In the tool sheds and potting sheds you will find evidence of Edwardian splendour – they had sixteen gardeners full time. In the kitchens, evidence of medieval slavery – the cook was fat and German and beat her eleven skivvies with her rolling pin (Victorian). The below-stairs quarters will be found under the roof – the amenities provided will appal you, but the stables will make you want to own a string of horses and ride across the distant downs every morning – on the days when you're not racing.

It is as well to remember at this juncture that the people who lived here couldn't afford it either, which is why they are selling up – unless they left the country to avoid death duties or something equally unpatriotic.

In the bedrooms, the magnificence of the ceilings will rival the polish on the parquet floors; in the drawing rooms, the dining rooms, the morning rooms, libraries and billiard rooms you will find the entire family heritage catalogued and numbered and exposed to the eyes of hundreds of connoisseurs – nine out of ten of whom will be hoping to send the lot to America.

On the last day of viewing you may catch a glimpse of the famous 'Ring' (*q.v.*). This manifestation will take the shape of five or six extremely disreputable characters in a huddle together, whispering and shaking their heads as though they were discussing something illegal in great secrecy. They give this impression because they *are* discussing something illegal in great secrecy. They are working out how best to lower the prices so that they can buy the goods cheaply.

St. Sothebys and St. Christies

As though entering a church, you should tip-toe into these sacrosanct premises with a solemn expression. That is all that is required of you apart from treating everyone with great respect. If the intense academic and antiquarian atmosphere is too much for you – leave.

There are several temples on these premises in which services are held at indeterminate times. A high priest stands in a pulpit with a hammer while a number of servers hold up other people's possessions for sacrifice.

The ritual is simple, quick and silent. No one but the high priest is allowed to talk, but certain members of the congregation are permitted to make offerings for the sacrifice. One's intention to make an offering is signalled in various ways: the bowing of the head, the shaking of the head, the nodding of the same, the closing of one eye or the sudden raising of the arm as though wishing to be excused.

When the high priest is satisfied that a suitable offering has been made he attempts to hit his thumb with the hammer.

The congregation member who is most generous is obliged to take the sacrifice away with him, whether he likes it or not. This could be awkward if it is a grand piano and he has come that day with only a plastic bag

Top auction rooms are a theatrical experience, a 'happening' in the truest form. Students of drama should attend regularly and watch the faces of the bidders. Antique collectors should also attend regularly as this is where they will get the best value, and genuine, antiques.

THE RING

George, Fred, Bert, Harry and Mrs. Posh-Socks (thus affectionately nicknamed by the Trade), are all antique dealers of one shape or another.

On a happy morning in May, or June, or any month you care to choose, these five individuals meet by chance at the viewing of a sale to be held at 'The Corbies', Upper Didsfold. The house is pseudo from top to bottom, but all the same has an old-world charm, due mainly to its surroundings at the end of a lovely postcard village, and its well-maintained garden laid out to lawn with roses galore.

In the house, the low-beamed drawing room is packed with neighbours who are curious to know what the late widow-owner left her daughter who emigrated six years ago and who prefers hard cash to handed-down sentimental knick-knacks.

Our five friends are now in the garage pretending like mad to be interested in an old petrol can. In fact they are discussing the Regency Period Mahogany Sofa Table (on Lyre-shaped supports having arched stretchers) hidden under Lots 46, 47 and 48 in the dining room. The item is in poor condition but could be restored and is worth at least £800.

They decide that they all want it for less, and are willing to risk up to £700 between them. They then pick George to do the bidding because he's the most likely to have a customer for it, and the auctioneer's suspicions must not be aroused.

The following day, at 11.30, George, the only one of the five attending the auction, puts in an opening bid of £40. This irritates the auctioneer who knows his job well and suspects the table is worth at least £400. He suggests a more realistic opening bid of £200.

An unexpected London dealer nods his head and a private buyer bids £210. George straight away puts in a bid of £300 scaring the wits out of the private buyer. The London dealer suggests £400. George runs him up to £480 and there is a pause. The villagers are excited. No one has ever paid so much money for a table before, and what a pity the widow-owner isn't alive to hear about it! '490' says the London dealer, and George caps it at £500. No one else bids. The auctioneer is annoyed. It is worth much more but none of the other local dealers seem to be there to compete. Reluctantly he ends the bidding. 'Going, going . . . gone!' The hammer comes down and George gets the table for £500. He shows no emotion at all but inside he is delighted.

In the bar of the local pub, our five meet the same evening. The purchase price of the sofa table was £500, so they each put in £100. The table now belongs to all of them, but George himself is rather keen to have it, so he says he'll pay £550. Harry (who has a collector-customer willing to pay at least £800 without a doubt) bids £600.

Mrs. Posh-Socks suggests £620 and Bert, who must make a bid or get out of the ring, mumbles £630. Fred, not interested, backs out. In so doing, Fred collects a share of the profit at that moment in time – the difference between £500 (the purchase price) and the £630 so far bid by the Ring. This is £130, a fifth of which is £26; he therefore collects £26 for having joined the Ring, plus the £100 he originally invested.

The bidding goes on. Bert backs out at £660 and collects £36, his share of the profit (a quarter of the difference between £500 and £660 as there are only four in the Ring). The table is finally bought by Harry for £700. George and Mrs. Posh-Socks each getting

£67, plus their original investment, as their share of the final profit.

Harry is happy, having got an £800 table for £700, the others are satisfied with having made a small profit on the side. Fred regrets not having stayed in the bidding a bit longer, thus getting more of the profit, but the others are pleased he didn't, or their share wouldn't have been as big.

Mrs. Posh-Socks sighs with relief. She likes to join the 'Ring' as it makes her feel professional, but she remembers how the professional dealers got the better of her when they first invited her in. On that occasion they told her a mahogany dumb waiter purchased for £70 was worth at least £300, and she had gladly bought it in the Ring auction for £250 thinking she had a bargain. The other members of the ring shared the £200 clear profit and she had found herself landed with a reproduction dumb waiter worth not more than £60.

'Ring' members are sharks; they are sharp enough to do something illegal and get away with it, quick-witted and mercenary enough to twist a fellow dealer if he's not on the ball.

The 'Ring' is a gamble for the members, a fair gamble, but unlike other gambles it has an innocent victim – the person selling the piece the 'Ring' bids for.

If you have something in an auction worth £1,000, and the 'Ring' is present, you are only likely to get £300 for it.

Very nasty.

DATES

Having imbibed the background to the Antique Trade in Great Britain, (similar on the Continent except that dealers get either more or less excited, depending on how close they are to the Mediterranean) we move on to the purer bits – knowledge which will enable you to outshine them all.

It is very much in your best interests to memorise the following dates and contemporary names.

Renaissance	**1450–1650**
Tudor	**1485–1603**
Henry VII	1485–1509
Henry VIII	1509–1547
Edward VI	1547–1553
Mary I	1553–1558
Elizabeth I	1558–1603
Stewart	**1603–1714**
James I	1603–1625
Charles I	1625–1649
Cromwell	
Commonwealth &	
Protectorate	1649–1660
Charles II	1660–1685
James II	1685–1688
William & Mary	1688–1694
William	1694–1702
Anne	1702–1714
In France: Louis XIV	1643–1715

Georgian	**1714–1800**
George I	1714–1727
George II	1727–1760
George III	1760–1820
In France: Louis XV	1715–1774
Louis XVI	1774–1793
Regency	**1800–1830**
George III	1760–1820
George IV	1820–1830
In France: Napoleon	1799–1814
Empire	1793–1830
Victorian	**1830–1901**
William IV	1830–1837
Victoria	1837–1901

TRUE ANTIQUES

Anything made after 1830 is not considered to be antique by the purists. You should therefore turn your nose up whenever anyone mentions William IV or Victoria in the same sentence as anything pre-George IV.

Your attitude towards anyone collecting Edwardiana should be one of amused disdain. If you are wise, however, you will quietly be collecting Edwardiana yourself: in twenty years' time anything Edwardian will be regarded as antique by those who decide such things. And they alone know who they are.

FURNITURE

Trees are regional. Certain trees only grow in certain areas of the world. These areas had to be discovered and the woods shipped to the countries who wanted them. All this took time and therefore the type of wood with which a piece of furniture is made is a primary indicator as to its date.

The walnut tree, for example, was not introduced into England before 1587. Therefore no English piece of furniture made of walnut is likely to be older than that date.

Woods used in antique furniture:—

DARK WOODS	Mahogany
	Oak
	Rosewood
	Walnut
	Yew
LIGHT WOODS	Applewood
	Beech
	Birch
	Elm
	Pine
	Satin Wood

Useful terms to face furniture with

Art Nouveau – Stiff vertical style of furniture. To be pronounced as in 'Ah, nouveau riche'.

Balluster – Turned pillar to support rail. See 'Turning'.

Baroque – Grotesque style developed in the 17th century.

Beading – Small semi-circular ridge.

Cornice – Upper projection on pieces of furniture.

Dentils – Guess what? Teeth under the cornice.

Fillet – Narrow strip. Not edible.

Finial – Knob on top of post.

Gadrooning –Edging of carved, identical, oval shapes. Also 12th Gadroons.

Japanning – Tea drinking ceremony or oriental glossy lacquer finish achieved by gum-lac dissolved in spirits.

Joinery – Work that has joints.

Marquetry – Inlay.

Mortise – Round peg in round hole.

Moulding –Raised ornamental band.

Ogee – Americanism for 'super'. Also concave/convex shape of a support.

Ormolu – Gilded metal mounts.

Patera – Classical oval disc struck on furniture.

Pediment – Ornamental structure surmounting cornice.

Plinth – Low base of a piece of furniture.

Reeding – Slim pipes, series of, as decoration.

Rococo – Overdone ornamental work of shells, scrolls, curves.

Splat – Ancient sign of annoyance by cabinet makers, as in 'He hit his thumb and splat'. Also middle of the back of chairs.

Stretcher – Horizontal bar joining chair legs.

Turning – Working wood with cutting tools as it rotates on a lathe.

The Tudor Period (1485-1603)

In 1485 Henry VII came to the throne. With his accession people became more civilised; that is to say they started using furniture, sleeping on beds, sitting on chairs and putting their things away neatly in boxes. This had nothing to do with Henry, it came about because the Italians were developing their Renaissance, a period during which foreigners produced lots of new and exciting ideas and became immensely prosperous, while Britain lagged behind. Rather like today.

Big houses had remarkably little furniture when the Tudors took over: a bed or two, benches, stools, tables, a couple of chairs maybe, but only the master and mistress of the house were allowed to sit on them. Large boxes of all shapes and sizes were popular and they served as seats, tables and sometimes beds. They are now called chests.

All such furniture was made of OAK.

The better pieces were crudely carved but often gilded and gaily painted. This helped to protect the wood against the damp and the insects. There was no glass in the windows and anything could walk in during the night.

By the time Henry VIII was crowned, things improved tremendously. Hell-bent on impressing foreigners and ladies, he dissolved the monasteries and used their money to build palaces and double beds. The carpenter came more into his own and the practice of joinery ousted heavy plank construction, in favour of panelling for walls. To carvings of the usual Gothic linenfold and Tudor Rose designs were added garlands and profiled heads in roundels, influenced by the Italian artists.

Elizabeth One then came to the throne and things improved even more. Furniture became really sophisticated and the nouveau-riche never stopped trying to outdo each other. Proof of status came with the use of the chisel. No bare surface on wall or furniture was safe – medallions, festoons of fruit, lozenges, eagles, naked boys; you imagine it, they chiselled it, and to top it all they invented the four-poster.

Obvious examples of Tudor furniture are:

PLANK CHEST: Box made of hewn planks strapped together with iron bands, the lid attached by wires to make hinges. Iron locks usually fitted. The sides, lower than the front and back, act as feet.

WAINSCOT CHAIR: Armchair on a box. Used only by the master of the house. The box on which the person sat was usually a locker – big enough to put a potty in.

GLASTONBURY CHAIR: A folding chair with elbowed arms. Until late in the 16th century all chairs had arms. Chairs without arms were regarded as stools with backs and were called Back Stools.

TRESTLE TABLE: Large rectangular board resting on uprights, or trestles, linked by a rail held in position by pegs. The board gave its name to 'Board and Lodging' meaning breakfast and bed. The tables were taken to pieces and stacked when the meal was over.

ELIZABETHAN DRAW TABLE: A massive table with a draw-leaf device for extending when called on unexpectedly for lunch. Huge bulbous legs, heavy carving round edge of top. One refers to them as Refectory Tables.

ELIZABETHAN POSTED BED: Usually known as the four-poster. Use of the right term will distinguish you from the rabble. Within four posts and a back, a bed frame made of cords stretched across to support the mattress. Remarkably uncomfortable.

DESK BOX: When printed books made their appearance, portable desks arrived. They are just like school desks without legs. When someone finally invented the legs the Desk Box became a school desk.

All these items were, of course, made of oak.

The Jacobean Period (1603 - 1625)

When James I was crowned they put the red carpet out for him. It was the first time a red carpet had ever been put out for anyone because it had only just been loomed. Up till then they had rush matting. James I also acquired a cushion to sit on, and after that furniture makers started upholstering their chairs. It was the beginning of comfort.

FARTHINGALE CHAIR: A single chair, or back stool, with high broad seat and low padded inclined back. The upholstery was handsomely embroidered and the chair is called farthingale because it showed to advantage the women's hooped and whaleboned dresses.

JACOBEAN LONG TABLE: A less elaborate type of refectory table than its Elizabethan predecessor. Some were so long they had to have eight legs. Though they were mostly made of oak, yew and elm were sometimes used.

Carolean Period (1625 - 1649)

When Charles I lost his head, he was no doubt consoled by the fact that the block was made of genuine oak. The Puritans reigned instead, and for ten years carpenters went back to making unamusing stuff, so farmhouse furniture replaced the comfort that people had begun to enjoy.

MORTUARY CHAIR: Pretty ordinary looking chair with an uncomfortable back carved to look like moustached masks portraying the head of Charles I. You have to know it was meant to be a moustached mask.

GATE-LEG TABLE: A round table with folding flaps. Also known as a falling table. If you sit at it suddenly, and are not careful where you put your knees, half the table will drop in your lap along with everything on it. There are many copies of this, but the originals had nails holding the hinges of the flaps. Elsewhere the joints were secured by oak pins.

The Restoration Period (1660 - 1688)

In 1660 Charles II and his court came over from France bringing with them the stunning ideas which Louis XIV had been dreaming up for Versailles.

In 1666 someone dropped a cigarette end in the city of London, and the whole lot went up in smoke.

Thus walnut and beach replaced oak, and foreign cabinet-makers flooded the market with the techniques of veneering, marquetry and lacquer. Things became so beautiful around the house that people stopped baiting bears in the market-place and started baiting each other in fashionable drawing rooms. They haven't stopped since.

CHARLES II CHAIRS: Exuberant S-scrolls flank the back panels with twist turning in flamboyant forms. Cane seats, front stretchers matching the cresting rail.

CAROLEAN DAY BED: Long version of the above. You could lie full length on it if you really wanted to be uncomfortable. Made after the Carolean age was over, just to confuse us.

PEPYSIAN BOOKCASE: Determined to be remembered in every field, Pepys had a bookcase made up for him, which was copied for others. It was made of solid oak with glass doors, in two sections, one tall cabinet resting on a chest-shaped cabinet. Carved frieze decorated the jutting-out cornice.

JAMES II DRESSER: Not to be outdone, James II had a dresser named after him. A typical kitchen or Welsh dresser, it stood on four legs, baluster turned, had three stretchers (none at the rear) and the three drawer fronts were decorated with a couple of 'panels'. The upper shelf was usually decorated with a primitive scalloped design. Genuine pieces have no back board.

William and Mary Period
(1689 - 1702)

This royal couple furnished their palaces with pieces designed by Dutch craftsmen who liked tied stretchers on chairs and domed tops for cabinets. Mary died in 1694 and William went on by himself and the whole of the period was unbelievably boring. But they left behind them some grand walnut furniture in the shape of:

WILLIAM & MARY STOOL: Upholstered in velvet, heavily carved legs and front stretchers, made to match the rest of the furniture in the drawing room. The sort of comfortable piece of furniture one cannot resist sitting on in front of the fire on Christmas day – if the cat hasn't already bagged it.

WILLIAM & MARY BUREAU CABINET: A desk with drawers, and a flap which opens down to reveal pigeon holes. Above the bureau is a cabinet with arched doors. The higher ceilings encouraged this sort of piece.

WILLIAM & MARY CHEST OF DRAWERS ON STAND: Speaks for itself. Walnut veneered, sometimes covered with marquetry.

The Queen Anne Period (1702 - 1714)

Queen Anne had cabriole legs. That is to say, thick and bandy. She was also very busy keeping cabinet makers busy. A mass of furniture was made in Queen Anne's time. And, as few people can tell the difference between late William & Mary, Queen Anne and early Georgian, it's a safe bet to say 'That's a fine example of Queen Anne.' Walnut, though; always walnut.

QUEEN ANNE CHAIR: Violin-shaped centre piece in a hoop forms the curving back, drop-in seat (that means you can take it out to re-cover), unstretched cabriole legs, ball and claw feet, scallop shell decoration at the top of the front legs, square back legs.

QUEEN ANNE GRANDFATHER CHAIR: High-backed winged easy chair, copied and re-copied by the Victorians. Period pieces, however, have needle-work upholstery, thoroughly worn.

QUEEN ANNE DRESSING TABLE: You can be caught out on this one. It's been reproduced by everyone, sometimes very badly. It's a walnut veneered table with drawers, and a knee-cracker posing as an arched-shaped frontpiece under the centre drawer.

The all important and much abused Georgian Period (1714 - 1800)

Cabriole legs became sturdier, very probably because George I was a man. Mahogany was imported from Cuba and carpenters thought it splendid because it was harder and crisper than walnut. And English worms didn't like the taste. Mahogany, therefore, is Georgian.

The majority of antiques, be they furniture, porcelain, glass or silver, date from this period. It is a well-studied and well-documented period and therefore safe; you can check up on everything. Antique collectors like safety and this is why they are always happy to buy 'Georgian'.

The Georgian period was the age of classical education. Those who could afford to send their poet sons abroad did so, getting Cooks to plan the Grand Tour. Some came back with new impressions and passed them on. Others came back drunk.

Houses were built carefully, grandly, with gardens to match, and the furniture and ornaments had to be of a very high standard to please the new fussy generation. The screws, for example, were all hand made.

Since the period is a safe and long one everybody hides their lack of knowledge behind it. You can do the same, and, turning your nose up ever so slightly at the mention of Georgian, get by with only a few well-chosen names and dates.

The following were all furniture designers of one sort or another and some, apparently, thought it necessary to become authors as well.

WILLIAM KENT   1686–1748.
THOMAS CHIPPENDALE   1718–1779.
The Gentleman and Cabinet Maker's Director.
ROBERT ADAM   1728–1792.
HENRY HOLLAND   1745–1806.
THOMAS CHIPPENDALE THE YOUNGER 1749–1822.
THOMAS SHERATON   1751–1806.
The Cabinet Maker's and Upholsterer's Drawing Book.
GEORGE HEPPLEWHITE   Died 1786.
The Cabinet Maker's and Upholsterer's Guide.
INCE AND MAYHEW   1759–1763.
Universal System of Household Furniture.
ROBERT MANWARING   18th century.
The Cabinet and Chair Maker's Real Friend and Companion and *The Chairmaker's Guide.*

The Regency Period (1800 - 1830)

Though Prince George was Regent from 1811 to 1820, the label 'Regency' is attached to any antique dating from the first thirty years of the 19th century. It is attached to Victorian reproductions too – but only by scurrilous or ignorant dealers.

During the Regency period designers were nearly all inspired by the French and their Napoleonic styles. Brass on wood was one of the main features, and upon seeing any brass embellishments you may well exclaim 'Ah, Regency'. Or if you wish to imply a note of continental antique knowledge, 'Ah, Empire'. The word 'Empire' however must not be pronounced as in British Empire (R.I.P.), but as in 'ampère', the unit of electric current.

Much of the original Regency furniture made to sit on was upholstered with Regency stripes. Stripes, therefore, are a fair indicator to the period. Whether this is imitation or genuine is up to you.

GRECIAN COUCH: A usual part of the well-to-do Regency interior. Ladies used to recline on them and have their hands asked for in marriage. They are now used in smart Harley Street consulting rooms by top psychiatrists.

PILLAR AND CLAW DINING TABLE: Single pillar with four splayed legs each with a brass wheel as a foot. Tables were supplied in units; you went on adding, depending on the number of guests you had for dinner.

DRUM TABLE: All kinds of round tables became popular in the Regency period; the drum, or capstan, was a table on a pillar with splayed legs, as above, and drawers fitted all round under the top.

TEAPOY: A tea chest standing on a small tripod table. The Regency ones became very ornamented with brass inlay and rosewood. It was fitted with three or four tea canisters and a couple of mixing bowls. No section was reserved for tea-bags.

CANTERBURY: A castored stand for sheet music or cutlery. The sheet music one became popular during the Regency period because that was when young ladies began to read music and bore everyone stiff while Mama poured tea from the teapoy. The piece consists of a drawer on wheels on top of which is fitted open-worked filing sections. Now in common use for storing the Sunday colour magazines.

The Victorian Period (1830 - 1901)

In previous periods everything was hand-made by craftsmen who lavished love and attention on what they were making. In the Victorian era the industrial revolution turned everyone machine-mad, and furniture was mass produced.

Reproductions came into their own and ruined everyone's taste and the craftsmen's initiative to invent. Though today Victorian copies of Queen Anne furniture are gaining value as antiques, and are much better made than the rubbish turned out as poor imitations of Victorian imitations, they are a very far cry from the genuine article.

The Victorian reproduction is *the* piece of furniture on which a dealer can lose money at an auction. They are difficult to recognise, some being cleverly made, but there can be a difference of several hundred pounds between the real thing and the adaptation.

Art Nouveau (c. 1880 - 1910)

A creative period of languishing, swooning artistic revival, coupled with a determined enthusiasm for decadence. It lasted twenty years, fired by the count-down to the end of the 19th century and the joyous birth of the 20th, Victoria-less.

Art Nouveau embodied the Flamboyant Gothic, Classical Antiquity, and the Moslem East with strong infiltrations of Japanese art.

Artists in every field suddenly rediscovered the meaning of Spring. Nature motifs, from exploding tulips to tenderly twining branches and stems, appeared everywhere.

'Superfluous', 'illegitimate', 'a phenomenon of impurity' will always be apt comments when studying a piece of Art Nouveau. And perhaps the best description of all is 'curvilinear anguish'.

Several names are essential. **Aubrey Beardsley,** usually referred to as the Prince of Art Nouveau who is best known for his erotic drawings in *The Yellow Book*; **René Lalique** who worked in anything three dimensional, from silver and opaline glass chalices, to gold moulded carved crystal and enamel brooches; **Louis Comfort Tiffany** who designed those draped bedside lamps; **Emile Gallé** who did wondrous things in glass, and **Antoni Gaudi** who can be credited with having fathered the word 'gawdy' with his architecture.

Art Deco (c. 1925)

In 1925 there was an explosive exhibition in Paris – *L'Exposition Internationale des Arts Decoratifs et Industriels Modernes* – from which none of us have really recovered.

Shortened to Art Deco, the movement gave young designers the excuse to revel against the floral excesses of Art Nouveau, and use rulers and set squares with a vengeance.

Art Deco is virtually everything created with straight lines between the two world wars, from automobile headlamps to cinema ashtrays. You are recommended to collect now to sell for a profit in the year 2001.

ORIENTAL CARPETS AND RUGS

CARPETS = Persian
RUGS   = Caucasian, Turkish, Turkomen
              and Chinese–Turkestan

When entering a carpetted or rugged room, always kick the corner of the floor-covering violently to expose the underside. Experts do this to look at the weave which immediately tells them whether it has a sehna or ghiordes knot. That in turn tells them all sorts of other things which must be important or they wouldn't do it.

ARMS AND ARMOUR

A wide and fascinating subject for warmongers and only to be studied if visiting a rich and military-minded uncle or retired General who may have a few bascinets, burgonets, cinquedas, falchions, musketons or petronels hanging on his walls.

The first two are helmets, the second two swords, the third two guns. Now you know what you're in for.

GLASS

There isn't all that much glass about, due entirely to the fact that glass breaks, and many have. The first thing to do when you pick up any glass is flick it nonchalantly with thumb and finger till it emits a resonant tone loud enough for the owner to wince.

The second is to feel the base for a possible pontil mark (*q.v.*); and finally you can turn your attention to the glass it's made of.

Early flint glass varied considerably in weight and clarity. Flint glass, now termed lead crystal, was made of silica from calcined flints. George Ravenscroft developed it round about 1674. Then in 1675 he used lead oxide instead of vegetable potash as a flux. This produced a glass cleaner, heavier and softer and with greater refractive brilliance than anything previously made. Hooray for Ravenscroft. Everything made since has merely been to try and improve on it.

The important Pontil Mark

If you're going to talk glass don't refer to the Pontil mark and Pontil, but as 'Punty'. Don't ask why.

The Punty (or Pontil) is the long iron rod attached to the end of blown glass during the finishing processes after removal from the blowpipe. This Punty mark (or Pontil mark) is the scar that it leaves when it's detached.

From 1750 onwards these scars were ground and polished into a smooth depression, but not always. From 1780 they always were.

So, if when feeling the base of any glass, you cut your finger with the sharp edge of a punty mark, you know that it must be an old glass certainly pre 1780, possibly pre 1750.

The decorative Knop

The swollen blob on the pillar or stem of a glass is a knop. There are many differently shaped knops, and here are some of the ones you could finger.

Acorn Knop – Shaped like an acorn, sometimes inverted.

Angular Knop – A round edged, flattened, knop, placed sideways.

Annulated Knop – A flat knop sandwiched between two, four or six flattened knops each pair progressively less in size.

Ball Knop – Large and spherical.

Bladed Knop – Thin, sharp edged knop, placed sideways.

Bullet Knop – Small, round, sometimes called an olive button.

Cylinder Knop – Cylindrical shaped, often containing a tear. (See *Tears* below).

Merese Knop – Sharp edged, connecting bowl and stem.

Quatrefoil Knop – A short knop pressed into four wings. The wings are upright or twisted.

Swelling Knop – A slight stem protuberence containing a tear.

The Tear

A bubble of air enclosed within the glass for decorative purposes, usually in the shape of a tear.

From 1715 to about 1760 clusters of spherical and tear-shaped tears appeared in bowl bases and knops.

A simple rule to keep in mind is that there is nothing before 1674 worth mentioning, tears between 1715 and 1760, and no knops after 1780.

Some glasses to ping and look through

ALE GLASS: Long, narrow flute for serving ale.

CORDIAL GLASS: Four to six-inch high. A long stem, topped with a small bowl, rather like a mini-lampost.

DRAM GLASSES: Also known as Nips, Joeys, Ginettes and Gin Glasses. Tiny, thick glasses with small bowls, big enough to hold, surprise, surprise – a dram.

GOBLET: Large bowl compared with stem height, capable of holding a gill (¼ pint), or more.

JACOBITE GLASSES: Cryptic glasses bearing emblems and mottoes for The Cause. Most common are the six-petalled Jacobite rose with one or two buds. The rose represents the House of Stewart, the small bud the Old Pretender, the large bud Prince Charles Edward's arrival in Scotland. Knowing your history helps you appreciate it all. Other Jacobite emblems include a stricken oak, an oak leaf, a bee, a butterfly, a carnation, a daffodil, three ostrich plumes and a thistle. In other words any glass bearing some sort of design could be Jacobite.

ROMER: 1675–1825. Not to to to be mistaken for Rummer. A pale green glass with a more or less spherical bowl with a slice taken off the top. Looks like a deformed goblet.

RUMMER: 1760–1850. Not to be mistaken for Romer. Short-stemmed drinking glass with capacious ovoid bowl on small foot. Hard to break, quite a number survive.

Further reading on the subject can only increase your fun. There are lots of words to learn, i.e. concerning stems alone, there are the following: *Air Twist, Baluster, Colour Twist, Compound Twist, Drawn, Facet Cut, Hollow, Incised, Knopped* (you know about that one), *Mercury Twist, Mixed Twist, Round the Twist.*

POTTERY AND PORCELAIN

You can't see through pottery. You can't see through porcelain either but it is transluscent – that is, if you hold it up to the light you can see the shadow of a finger through it. Very uncanny.

There are three accepted forms of pottery and porcelain: English, Continental and Chinese.

Pottery is usually fairly thick and heavy; porcelain can be very light and dainty.

Porcelain is made in two forms, *soft paste* and *hard paste.* It is important to find out which paste a piece of porcelain is made of for this is an instant indicator as to where it comes from. Hard paste is Continental, soft paste is English, (as a rule).

To tell the difference between the two, a nail file should be sawn into the base of any piece of porcelain; if you manage to make an impression without too much effort, then the paste is soft. If you are incapable of making any impression at all, blunt the nail file or drop the piece because you've applied too much pressure, the piece is hard.

An amateur collector can be spotted a mile off by the way he handles porcelain. The professional can likewise be recognised. A piece of pottery or porcelain should always be approached with a certain amount of ruthlessness; you must not be frightened of dropping it. The impression, at all times, must be given that if you *do* drop it, it doesn't matter because you can always buy the pieces.

To achieve this confidence (you need confidence when lifting a £5,000 Han Dynasty stoneware pot from a high shelf in a famous saleroom), practise with plastic plates at home.

Always lift a valuable piece with two hands, placing one hand at the bottom and one hand on the top, at the same time checking that the head, the lid, or any other extra part is firmly held. If the lid is removable, remove it.

Once the piece is firmly held in both hands examine it with a smirk, then turn it upside down abruptly to look at the mark. The mark will tell you all, that is if you have a computer memory. If you haven't got a computer memory, it won't tell you a thing. There are approximately 1,500 ceramic marks to remember. And if you don't know what ceramics is, ceramics is pottery and porcelain.

It is impolite to drop other people's pieces of pottery or porcelain. Drop these terms instead.

Biscuit – Fired but unglazed pottery or porcelain.

Bocages – Foliages or tree backgrounds to pottery or porcelain figures.

Earthenware – Pottery made of baked clay, generally heavy and crude.

Glaze – Glassy material applied to earthenware and porcelain which makes it waterproof and smooth to touch. Glaze is versatile for it can be dull or matt or brilliant colours.

Ironstone – A white earthenware alleged to contain slag.

Japan – An oriental pattern and style.

Lustre – Decoration on pottery or porcelain made with thin films of metal. A metallic look.

Slip – Clay reduced to a liquid applied as an extra coating on pottery for decorative purposes. Hence the old saying 'There's many a slip 'twixt cup and lip'.

Stone China – A hard white pottery made as a cheap substitute to porcelain.

ENGLISH POTTERY

BRISTOL: 1683-1770. Early Bristol is like Lambeth. Late Bristol is like Liverpool. So don't comment on Bristol, Lambeth or Liverpool; you might make a fool of yourself or worse, if right, make a fool of the collector. Unforgivable.

DAVENPORT: 1793. Cream coloured earthenware. Also name of Georgian small writing desk with characteristic set of drawers pulling out sideways. The two have no connection.

DENBY: 1833. Brown stoneware.

DERBYSHIRE: Indistinguishable from Nottingham.

DOULTON: 1818. Brown stoneware.

FULHAM: 1670-1693. Huge brown and grey mugs with applied reliefs depicting hunting scenes.

LAMBETH: See *Bristol.*

LEEDS: 1750. Frequently enamelled creamware. Pierced decorations, also figures.

LIVERPOOL: See *Lambeth.*

MASON: 1813. Ironstone china. Usually blue and red. The name is written in full on the bottom of plates and mugs. You can't go wrong, but neither can anyone else.

MINTON: 1756–1836. The willow pattern people. Blue painted pottery – also porcelain. Much reproduced, so beware.

NOTTINGHAM: See *Derbyshire.*

PRATT WARE: Late 18th Early 19th. Lead glazed pottery mainly in brown, orange, blue and green. Also red, yellow, indigo and violet.

ROCKINGHAM: 1750–1806. Similar to Leeds but distinctive streaky dark brown glaze. Also porcelain.

STAFFORDSHIRE: To say that a piece of pottery is Staffordshire will not be wrong; most potters worked in Staffordshire. That's why the area is known as the Potteries. Useful names to hand around: Adams, Astbury, Daniel, Greatbach, Hollins, Mason, Palmer, Ridgeway, Turner, Wedgewood, Whieldon and Wood.

TOBY JUGS: Originally made by one Ralph Wood, hundreds of other potters have copied them. Best line to deliver when breaking one, 'It wasn't an original Ralph Wood anyway'. Unless, of course, it was.

WALTON: 1820–1830. Small earthenware figures with background of flowers.

WEDGEWOOD: 1730–1795. Pick any bit of pottery up and say its Wedgewood – you may be right. Anything from green and yellow cauliflower wares to silver lustre.

ENGLISH PORCELAIN
(Soft Paste)

If by now you have not given up the idea of antique collecting, then you should go, like a bull, into a china shop and ask to see examples of the following. Either that or buy the hundreds of specialised books on the subject which will muddle you up no end. The following porcelain factories were established when stated:

BOW	1750
BRISTOL	1749
CAUGHLEY	1772
CHELSEA	1745
COALPORT	1780
DERBY	1751
LIMEHOUSE*	1750
LIVERPOOL	1710
LONGTON HALL	1750
LOWESTOFT	1737
NANTGARW	1813
PINXTON	1796
ROCKINGHAM	1820
(porcelain) Cottages a favourite.	
WORCESTER	1745

* Good talking point this one. The factory was short-lived. It was founded in 1750. Its products are unidentified, so wherever you are and whenever you see a bit of porcelain you're not sure of, say 'Limehouse'. No one can contradict you.

CONTINENTAL PORCELAIN
(Hard Paste)

MEISSEN*	1710	German
HOECHST	1750	German
BERLIN	1752	German
NYMPHENBURG	1753	German
FRANKENTHAL	1755	German
LUDWIGSBURG	1758	German
ZURICH	1763	Swiss

The brighter bluffer will have noted that except for Zurich, all hard paste porcelain seems to come from Germany. Remember this.

SÈVRES, often referred to as Vincennes, in France, was established in 1738. Though regarded as a Continental porcelain, it is made of *soft paste*. In 1769, however, they started making porcelain with a hard paste. So French porcelain should be mentioned with care.

Hard paste Porcelain factories in England, just to balance things evenly, are easy to remember. They are: PLYMOUTH, BRISTOL and NEW HALL.

* Meissen porcelain is often referred to as Dresden; this is because the Meissen factory was near Dresden. Meissen (or Dresden) is important because it was the first porcelain made in Europe.

CHINESE POTTERY AND PORCELAIN

China was first made in China. Naturally.

The Chinese made pottery years and years before we were born, about 2000 B.C., and invented Porcelain during the T'ang Dynasty; that's between 618 A.D. and 906 A.D. Dynasties are hurled around wholesale when talking Chinese China, so remember these:

SHANG-YIN	1766–1122 BC
CHOU	1122–249 BC
HAN	206 BC–AD 220
SIX DYNASTIES	220–589
T'ANG	618–906
FIVE DYNASTIES	907–960
SUNG	960–1279
YUAN	1279–1368
MING	1368–1644
CH'ING	1644–1912

You will note that the famous Ming Dynasty which everyone bandies about, is equivalent to our Tudor, Jacobean and Carolean furniture periods.

Other highly mentioned names connected with Chinese China are the colour families:

FAMILLE NOIRE ⎫	
FAMILLE VERTE ⎬	1662–1722
FAMILLE ROSE	1723–1735

All three belong to the Ch'ing Dynasty.

SILVER

The collector daft enough to decide on silver as a main interest in antiques will land up with a load of research work, polishing and frustration – unless very rich. Collecting silver was always an expensive hobby; today it is nearly prohibitive.

English silver survives from the 16th century in great quantities for two reasons. One: silver is money and therefore it has always been well looked after. Two: it is comparatively indestructible.

It has, of course, one redeeming feature, that of increasing in value continually. Buy some silver today and you can sell it at a profit tomorrow – provided you know what you're doing. If you don't, then don't sell.

The trouble with silver is its sheer quantity, and the very many different types in existence.

Leaving Continental silver aside completely, there are first of all the national divisions: **English** silver, **Scottish** silver and **Irish** silver.

Within the national divisions there are the periods: late 16th century English, 17th century Scottish, Early 18th century Irish etc. . . . and within the periods, there are the different styles of the different silversmiths. Within the categories of styles and silversmith there are the different types of objects they specialised in, and then there are the different categories of weight, and so on.

As with all other sections of antique collecting, silver has a language all to itself. Where in furniture one talks of beading, moulding and turning, and in pottery and porcelain one murmurs about glazing and hard and soft pastes, in silver one talks freely of *gadrooning, ovolo* and *wrigglework*.

(NB: words like *beading, gadrooning* and *fluting* are used in other than silver work but don't always mean the same thing.)

When handling a footed waiter (a flat cakestand object with a pedestal that usually has place of honour on the sideboard under a heap of wax fruit), first be careful not to leave your fingermarks all over the mirror-clean surface. Then comment on the fine pricking (delicate needle-point engraving). All this before turning it over to look at the all important hallmark.

No silver collector worth his octagonal trencher salt (1724) is ever seen without an eyeglass. This essential piece of equipment should, of course, be made of silver and be found deep down in one of your pockets, with difficulty.

When the eyepiece has been fixed firmly in the eye the hallmark should be examined and a grunt grunted. The eyepiece should then be released so as to fall into the pocket held open with the free hand.

It is now that you make a short comment. 'Mary Chawner and George W. Adams did their best work in that style,' will suffice. If the piece was indeed smithed by Mary Chawner and W. Adams you score 100. If it wasn't, you still score 100 for not having committed yourself to saying that it *was*. There are about 350 silversmiths whose names you could mention – if you were that sort of person.

Hallmarks

Four marks are usually found stamped on silver: the *hall,* or town, mark; the *maker's* mark; the *annual* mark or date letter; the *standard* mark, indicating the sterling quality.

As there are more than 2,000 permutations of these marks, we only propose to list the key marks for the halls, or towns.

LONDON: Leopard's Head Crowned. 1558–1716.
Britannia. 1716–1719.
Leopard's Head Crowned. 1719–1836.
Leopard's Head Uncrowned. 1836–Present.

BIRMINGHAM: Anchor.

CHESTER: Three wheatsheaves with a sword.

DUBLIN: Crowned harp.

EDINBURGH: Three-towered castle.

EXETER: Roman capital letter 'X', sometimes crowned for 16th and 17th centuries. After that, damnit, three-towered castle, as for Edinburgh.

GLASGOW: Tree, fish and bell (city arms).

NEWCASTLE: Three separate castle towers.

NORWICH: Castle over a lion passant (or a lion passing by with its right leg clawing the air).

SHEFFIELD: Crown. But, between 1815 and 1819 they stamped it upside down. The fools!

YORK:
Half leopard's head, half fleur de lys. 1562–1631.
Half rose crowned, half fleur de lys. 1632–1698.
Cross with five lions passant. 1700 on.

If you still wish to continue an insane interest in silver, your troubles can be greatly reduced by specialising in a particular form. We list below some more interesting silversmith's wares.

Almsdish. Asparagus tongs. Biggins. Blackjacks. Bleeding bowls. Caudle-cup. Censer. Chafing dish. Chalice. Chocolate pot. Ciborium. Communion cup (usually stolen). Douters. Ecuelle. Epergne. Freedom Box. Monteith. Muffineer. Papboat (for babies). Pomander. Porringer. Pouncebox. Quaich. Sandbox. Voyding dish. Waxjack.

And the following types of spoon:

Apostle, basting, caddy, dessert, egg, gravy, lion sejant, maidenhead (!), marrow, mulberry, mustard, olive, puritan, rat-tail, salt, seal-top, slip-top, snuff, straining (mulberry) stumptop, table, tea, tray, trifid, writhen top.

PEWTER

Pewter is an alloy, the principal commodity of which is tin, with minor additions of brass, lead and antimony.

The Romans started the pewter fad in Britain and by 1503 it was so popular that someone decided each bit of pewt should have its maker's mark – and it's not called a mark, but a 'touch'.

These 'touches' were recorded in the Pewterers Hall, London, which was burnt down in the Great Fire so all recordings of touches previous to 1666, aren't.

They rebuilt the Pewterers Hall, however, and since then 'touches' have been recorded.

ENAMELS

A variety of glass which when heated may be applied by fusion to metallic surfaces, either to decorate them in colours, or to form a surface that can be painted, or simply as a protection for cooking utensils.

The centre of enamelling since the Middle Ages has been Limoges. But take a staunchly patriotic line by praising England's own products from Battersea and South Staffordshire. It was the Swiss who perfected the art of painting highly intricate scenes in the 19th century to sell to tourists.

One of the most ancient forms of enamelling was Cloisonné (pronounced Klwah-zone-ay) which is recognised by the raised metal strips that make up panels into which the various coloured enamels are melted. Very expensive.

MINIATURES

When you spot the portrait of a minified female, and her face is pretty, you should say through a sigh 'Ahh, another unknown lady.'

Miniature artists (who were not necessarily small but painted in a small way) never seem to have known the women they painted — which leads one to imagine the worst . . . or best.

Holbein was the first fashionable artist to mini-paint in 1532. These miniatures were sometimes called limmings.

There are as many miniaturists as there are watercolour artists and the only thing to bear in mind is that the Victorians (as always) went mad and overdid their reproduction, covering walls with them because they liked to have people around. When someone invented the camera, they got rid of all their unknown female relatives, so those that survive have a certain value. These are painted on vellum or very thin ivory, and the frames are an indication of their date – provided you can find a way of telling if it's the original frame.

Try watercolours.

DRAWINGS AND PRINTS (Old English)

Drawings are pictures drawn with pencil, pen and ink, black or red charcoal or chalk, or dry-washed with indian ink in grey, blue or sepia.

A print is a drawing or painting transferred to a copper or zinc plate, a block of wood or a stone. The word 'print' applies to several methods: line engraving, etching, soft ground etching, drypoint, aquatint, mezzotint and lithography.

It is rather important if you're going to take an interest in this field to know a bit about each – at least the difference between them.

The big names to bandy about, are – *Constable, Gainsborough* and *Rowlandson* – in such remarks as 'It's not a Constable, Gainsborough or Rowlandson.'

OIL PAINTINGS

To become an expert, you will have to learn about canvases, paint pigments, depicted scenes, brush strokes, frame-manship and artists' signatures. When you've done all that you'll be about a hundred and thirty and may not care. So try watercolours.

WATER COLOURS

Few people talk water colour because it's boring and you need to have pretty good eyesight to appreciate one hanging in someone's drawing room, so it is very possible to become one of the few people who can know something about it.

Never consider anything painted before 1770 or after 1830, and show extreme disapproval if anyone mentions any water colour artist who is not English. Scottish artists might just be acceptable, but anything beyond Calais is definitely out.

There are ten names to remember. And what they've been known to paint.

COPLEY FIELDING	Seascape
COTMAN	Eton College
COX	Sheep on bridge in Wales
COZENS	Swiss mountain scene
DE WINT	Cumberland water mill
GIRTIN	Romantic landscape
HAVELL	Windermere landscape
PROUT	Caen, river, cathedral, people
TURNER, J. M. W.	Interiors of Salisbury Cathedral
VARLEY	Thames at Chiswick

SILHOUETTES

Etienne de Silhouette invented them. He was Louis XV's Finance Minister and cut out for the job.

FINAL BID

When talking to a collector or dealer about antiques you have bought always *halve* the price actually paid for anything, unless selling, of course. It is lunacy to admit that you purchased something for more than it was worth, and everything today is priced more than it is worth.

Below are listed actual prices paid in various auction rooms during 1984-85, for use as a rough guide.

1910 HMV 'Mellon Gramophone needle Tin'.	£3
1937 Cigarette Card series of 50 Aeroplane markings.	£6
Circular single sided enamel sign: 'Lyons Cakes'.	£15
Pair of George III Irish silver cast sugar tongs.	£22
Victorian helmet-shaped copper coal bucket.	£60
Late 19th century toy model Haywain in wood.	£106
19th century Dutch pewter wine flagon	£276
German 16th century leaded stained glass rosette.	£352
19th century Eastern hardwood veneered card table.	£600
T'ang dynasty, blue splashed straw glazed buff pottery broad oviform jar.	£1,080
Mid 16th century Nuremberg foot soldier's armour with burgonet helmet.	£3,300.
Late 18th century George III marble top console table.	£6,233
Two manual harpsichord in mahogany case by Jack and Abraham Kirckman. 1779.	£22,000
A Ch'ien Lung famille rose vase.	£36,720
Miniature of Jane Broughton aged 21, painted on vellum by Nicholas Hilliard. 1574.	£75,000
Spider web leaded glass mosaic and bronze table lamp by Tiffany.	£163,000
High marquetry and ormolu Louis XV corner cabinet by Dubois.	£844,440
Suit of armour by Giovanni Negroli for Henry II of France. 1545.	£1,925,000
'L'Attente' by Degas. Oil on canvas.	£2,413,000.

THE AUTHOR

André Launay is a French novelist who was born and educated in England and can only write in English. He has a Spanish wife, two grown-up sons who are bi-lingual, and a five year old daughter who is tri-lingual. This makes life somewhat confusing.

He is the well-known author of *The Girl With a Peppermint Taste* and *The Innocence Has Gone, Daddy,* neither of which won the Booker Prize. He has also had considerable success with a series of psychic horror books which were written under a pseudonym as being too horrible to acknowledge.

A compulsive collector of Antiques, he once ran an up-market junk shop in Somerset, during which time he acquired a valuable collection of Victorian dolls. His small daughter's lack of appreciation for their value forced him to give them up. He now collects turn of the century moulded brass bookends.

What André Launay does not know about antiques is not included in the pages of this volume.